Student-Centered Teaching for Increased Participation

James Kelly

nea PROFESSIONAL LIBRARY
National Education Association
Washington, D.C.

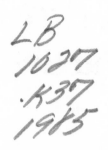

Copyright © 1985
National Education Association of the United States

Note

The opinions expressed in this publication should not be construed as representing the policy or position of the National Education Association. Materials published as part of the Reference & Resource Series are intended to be discussion documents for teachers who are concerned with specialized interests of the profession.

Library of Congress Cataloging in Publication Data

Kelly, James.
   Student-centered teaching for increased participation.

   (Reference and resource series)
   Bibliography: p.
   1. Activity programs in education—Handbooks, manuals, etc. 2. Motivation in education—Handbooks, manuals, etc. I. Title. II. Series.
LB1027.K37   1985   371.3'028   84-29503
ISBN 0-8106-1527-4

CONTENTS

To my parents . . .

and their respect for education,

and

to my wife, Bronwen, . . .

for her unending love, guidance,

support, and inspiration.

PREFACE

The idea for this book grew out of a sense of commitment: to my students, to my profession, to myself. I wanted to give my students the motivation and creative opportunities afforded me by several key educators in my life. An analysis of the style of these individuals led to a specific approach that I have endeavored to follow throughout my teaching career. This approach relies on student-centered activities to combat boredom and lack of motivation. I have found it to be extremely successful and rewarding; hence this book.

The emphasis here is on practicality. Far too much material written for teachers is highly philosophical in nature; it leaves them with the problem of what to do for tomorrow's lesson. *Student-Centered Teaching for Increased Participation* provides teachers with specifics to make their lessons more enjoyable, more creative, and more effective.

The book is divided into two sections. Part I intro-

duces teachers to the student-centered approach with a rationale, a description of the salient factors of student-centered activities, and an account of the technique I devised with this philosophy in mind. Part II is a collection of practical strategies that teachers can use tomorrow, if need be.

Although there are far too many dedicated people to thank individually, I would like to express my appreciation to a notable few. Many thanks to Anne Tallman whose comments and constructive criticism were essential in the preparation of this book. I would also like to pay tribute to those educators who made a difference in my life: Sister Francis Regis of St. Joseph's, Hilo, Hawaii; William Todt of Keyport High School, New Jersey; William Meisner of Jersey City State College; Dr. David Weischadle of Montclair State College, New Jersey; and Dr. Ken Job of William Paterson College, Wayne, New Jersey.

The Author

James Kelly teaches seventh and eighth grade social studies in the Richard Butler School, Butler, New Jersey.

The Advisory Panel

Joseph Bondi, College of Education, University of South Florida, Tampa

Michael E. Crane, Head Teacher, Pomona School, Galloway Township, New Jersey

Jeff Golub, English and speech teacher, Shorecrest High School, Seattle, Washington

Thomas W. Hine, Jr., sixth grade teacher, Wolcott School, West Hartford, Connecticut

Beverly G. Kinnischtzke, Home Economist, Ashley High School, North Dakota

Sharron A. Knechtel, Chapter I Head Teacher, Alhambra Schools, Phoenix, Arizona

Thomas Ousley, English teacher, Jennings School District, Missouri

Charles Ward, Special Education teacher, Hudson Middle School, North Carolina

PART I

Guide to Appendices

The Student-Centered Approach

RATIONALE OF
STUDENT-CENTERED APPROACH

I hear, and I forget;
I see, and I remember;
I do, and I understand.

—Chinese Proverb

The nation's schools are currently going through a critical phase of development. Various pressure groups are exerting influence to shape the schools according to their own needs and interests. Legislatures continue to increase their authority over the educational process, while boards of education, journalists, and others continue to push-pull the system in their own directions. The result is an amalgam of philosophies vying for control of the destiny of the schools.

Whatever direction the schools may take, one overriding consideration remains unchanged. The person who has to accept responsibility for what goes on in the classroom is the teacher. It is the teacher who is on the firing line, the teacher who has the responsibility for deciding how to teach a subject.

Kenworthy perhaps said it best when he described the job of a competent instructor:

> The job of the teacher is to discover every possible method for arousing interest, encouraging inquiry, stimulating questions, and promoting deep thinking. The superior teacher examines ideas, issues, problems, countries, people and institutions with students as if they were being placed under a magnifying glass. Real teaching, real learning, is the process of probing, discovering, analyzing, and examining. (8, p. 41)*

If educators accept this definition, they must examine the type of activities they select for use in the classroom. "How" teachers say or do something is often more important than "what" they say or do. Their methodology, then, should reflect the change of emphasis from curriculum to process by a careful selection of student-centered activities.

Teachers cannot view students as the receptacles of their vast store of knowledge. Again, to cite Kenworthy:

> Teaching is not primarily telling, or pouring information into pupils. Teaching is probing, discovering, analyzing, and examining under the guidance of a competent person. (8, p. 41)

Creating the right kind of atmosphere is paramount for any teacher who wishes to increase student participation. Students need the freedom to explore within a controlled environment. This freedom does not have to be synonymous with chaos. With proper guidance and discipline, children can flourish in a student-centered environment that remains within the parameters set by the teacher. To achieve such an atmosphere, the teacher must first establish him/herself "in control." Then, once the rules have been set up, the boundaries of student interest and participation are limitless.

Teacher or student can initiate the activities, as long as the teacher guides the student. This means a sharing of control, not an abdication—in other words, constructive student interaction in an atmosphere that is comfortable, yet controlled. The key is letting students know how far they can go.

Throughout this process, teacher input is crucial. Adopting a student-centered approach to teaching is by no means a way of abandoning teacher responsibility. Only within a properly guided framework can this encouragement of student participation have any true meaning. As Dewey points out, "... there are a multitude of ways of reacting to surrounding conditions, and without some guidance from experience these reactions are sure to be casual, sporadic, and ultimately fatiguing." (14).

It is important also to encourage children to become responsible for their learning. This implies a sharing of the authority that teachers enjoy. According to Coleman:

> Modern adolescents are not content with a passive role ... if a group is given no authority to make decisions and take action on its own, the leaders show no responsibility to the larger institution. Lack of au-

---

*Numbers in parentheses appearing in the text refer to the Bibliography on page 48.

thority carries with it lack of responsibility; demands for obedience generate disobedience as well. But when a person or group carries the authority for his own action, he carries responsibility for it. (6, p. 316)

The best way to teach students a sense of responsibility is to let them experience it. And there is no better way to do this than with an array of teaching activities geared toward student participation.

CHARACTERISTICS OF STUDENT-CENTERED ACTIVITIES

A brief description of the salient features of student-centered activities follows. These characteristics seem to be evident in most activities that increase student participation. Therefore they can serve as evaluation criteria for additional strategies to stimulate student involvement.

1. *The ability to create.* An outstanding feature of many of the activities examined in formulating this book was the option for students to create. As Anderson noted:

> In children, creativity is a universal. Among adults, it is almost non-existent. The great question is: What has happened to this enormous and universal human resource? This is the question of the age and the quest of our research. (2, p. xii)

When given the option to create as opposed to merely absorb, student participation increases markedly.

2. *Divergent rather than convergent thinking.* Convergent thinking is the process of teaching toward an already established answer. While few would argue the importance of identifying objectives and an organized plan for reaching them, the question of alternative routes arises. Or better, should one be headed in a particular direction at all?

For example, in teaching about World War II, one objective might be to show how the Allies were victorious. Why not also include, or perhaps substitute, the objective of trying to determine if the war should have been fought at all? The teaching of the unit could then center around, not converge toward, the question "Can World War II Be Justified?" (See Appendix 1.)

This approach lends itself to a divergent thinking process. As Renzulli defined it, "Divergent production is a kind of thinking that is characterized by a breaking away from conventional restrictions on thinking and letting one's mind flow across a broad range of ideas and possible solutions to a problem." (10, p. 3).

Such an approach allows students the opportunity to expand their minds by thinking in broader terms.

3. *Exercising curiosity and being allowed to act upon it.* Too often a child's curiosity is dampened by a teacher saying, "We aren't there yet" or "We have to do this first." By using the model that follows and by incorporating many of the activities described in Part II into a repertoire of teaching strategems, teachers can channel students' curiosity into productive results.

4. *Allowing for a free exchange of ideas.* Many of the activities described in Part II allow for student interaction in large or small groups. This technique is, and should be, a basis for any successful inquiry-based program.

5. *Sharing of control.* Some may view the model and activities described in this book as an abdication of control by the teacher. This may or may not be true. A teacher who "rules" a class as a strict authoritarian certainly would have to give up a bit of power. This does not, however, mean yielding control. The fear of surrendering one's authority to chaos is simply unfounded. The sharing of some power with students can mean greater rewards to be reaped—for example, a rise in the personal interest, and hence self-motivation, of individual students.

6. *A feeling of success in accomplishing a task.* There is no better way to ensure student motivation and interest than by increasing their chances of success.

7. *Varying resources.* Many of the activities described in this book require resources other than the traditional text. The use of these additional resources—library, community, other students, other faculty members—helps students become more involved in learning.

8. *Helping/working with others.* Many of the activities discussed in Part II encourage peer assistance, a goal of society, which should be a part of every program. In fact, when asked the most important thing they learned after completing a project, all members of a student group responded, "Learning to work with others."

9. *Exploring the affective domain.* Students are not only thinking beings, they are feeling beings. Consequently, they are often willing to participate in activities that—

    a. Help them express their feelings.
    b. Help them understand their values.
    c. Help them understand the feelings and values of others.

Many teachers will be able to identify other characteristics that will increase student involvement, particularly as they explore the activities in Part II.

MODEL

The model that follows is based on the foregoing characteristics. This model can be used in the classroom with maximum input of both teacher and student. Both can establish objectives but these will differ in substance. The objectives set by the teacher will be affective in nature. For example:

1. To establish an atmosphere that will be conducive to—

    a. The release of creativity.
    b. Student interaction.
    c. Student success.

2. To allow students the opportunity to—

    a. Explore varied resources.
    b. Work with peers.
    c. Share control with the teacher.

The objectives decided upon by the students, on the other hand, will be cognitive in nature and related to the topic of study. More about these later.

The technique begins with the selection of a concept. The teacher and/or students or the dictates of the curriculum make this decision. In History it may be "National Interest"; in Home Economics, "World Hunger"; in Science, "Environmental Problems." Please note that the activity can be easily adapted to any subject matter and most age groups. Also note that the activity can and should be one of several strategies used in studying the concept.

The next step is to have students form small groups of four or five. Make every effort to prevent the possibility of unpopular students working alone. For example, set a minimum number of workers for each group, use teacher-assigned groups, or devise a way to match students.

After the formation of the small groups, each group selects a leader and a recorder. The job of the group leader is to—

1. Make sure there is enough work for all group members.
2. Verify that all group members are working.
3. Report any group problems or considerations to the teacher.

Each group then receives a "Group Work Information Sheet" (see Appendix 2), which the recorder fills out in consultation with the other group members. This becomes a very important task, for it serves as the plan of action for the remainder of the activity. Students must pay very close attention to the section "Questions/Subtopics." Here they are given much latitude in deciding which way they want to go. They are, in effect, asking themselves: "What do I want to learn about this concept?" As a result of this process, they will develop a series of questions/subtopics emanating from student concerns. If these are slow in coming, an examination of the

text or other available information on the subject (and some teacher assistance) will be helpful. The questions/subtopics are recorded in the appropriate space on the worksheet and become the focus of the group's activities.

The group task is to explore these questions/subtopics by doing research. To facilitate this part of the process, students can collect appropriate sources from the library and work at group tables or gathered desks in the classroom. In my school, for example, the librarian allows us to keep the research data in the classroom for the duration of the activity. It is amazing how this simple change in the room's physical appearance—increased library materials stacked on the windowsill, desks arranged in groups instead of rows—encourages even hard-to-motivate students to work enthusiastically.

The ultimate goal of this endeavor is for students to share the fruits of their labor with the rest of the class. They do this by deciding upon and planning a series of activities that incorporate and illustrate the information they have accumulated in their research. They list these activities in the appropriate section of the "Group Work Information Sheet." Providing each group with a list of teaching techniques will greatly aid students in this task (see Appendix 3). (For a sample of the type of activities chosen by some of my students to deal with the "Annexation of Hawaii" and the "Spanish-American War," see Appendices 4 and 5.)

Finally, teacher and students must work out a time limit. Generally I allow approximately three weeks for students to do their research and one week to make their presentations. This time limit, it must be noted, is an estimate. Sometimes we exceed the limit, depending on students' progress. With a realistic approach on the part of students and a little assistance from the teacher, most time estimates can be met.

In an atmosphere that encourages creativity, the results of such an activity can be very impressive. The technique is not without its problems, however. For example, some students need more guidance than others. Teachers can help these students select worthwhile activities. Sometimes everyone may seem to need assistance at the same time. Teachers can avoid this situation by teaching the technique first and encouraging group members to help each other. Some groups may need more time than others. To accommodate them, a series of extra credit or enrichment assignments can be available to those groups that finish ahead of schedule. Another problem may occur when the activities of some groups do not meet the teacher's expectations. In such cases it is important to view the results in light of the students' overall accomplishments.

Evaluating student work is difficult and often subjective, especially when dealing with student-centered activities. But this technique lends itself to a variety of evaluative tools, all of which can be used effectively.

A criterion-referenced test for each group would be almost impossible. For a test on the completed unit (which includes this model as only one strategy among many), however, certain general questions may be used. For example:

1. Did you enjoy the group work? Why or why not?
2. What changes would you suggest to make the group work more enjoyable?
3. In your estimation, what is the most important thing you learned while participating in the group work?

Using questions like these on a test to evaluate the proficiency of learned data gives students an opportunity to practice the higher order thinking skills. For example, to answer the questions they must analyze their experience and their reactions to it, and justify their reasoning.

Another type of evaluation, the checklist, should be used throughout the group work experience (see Appendix 6). It should reflect certain concerns of both teacher and students such as—

1. The objectives
2. The activities
3. The availability of resources
4. The group experience itself.

A student–teacher conference is a must, in my estimation. Here, the teacher and students have an opportunity to clarify misconceptions and evaluate performances in a relaxed, open discussion format. Since most groups will finish their work at varying times, a conference can take place immediately upon completion of their projects. Teacher questions can include the following:

1. What are some of the things you learned while doing this project? (At this point it is a good idea to make a list by brainstorming and then place it in the group's folder.)
2. What, in your opinion, was the most important thing you learned?
3. Did you enjoy the group work? Why or why not?
4. How could we improve the group work?

During such a conference, many unintended learning outcomes emerge that can be essential in helping teachers understand their students and plan for the future.

And last, but certainly not least as an evaluative criterion, is the finished product itself, the result of the collaborative effort mentioned earlier—the specific activities each group has developed to present to the class. A good way to ensure the participation and attentiveness of class members viewing these presentations, as well as to provide a more reasonable base for teacher grading, is to use an evaluation sheet (see Appendix 7). I make absolutely sure beforehand, however, that students understand that my evaluation is the one that counts toward their grade. Most students, with a little prodding, will take this part of the procedure seriously. Sometimes they are harder on their peers than the teacher is.

Perhaps for the first time, many students when using this technique are being given tremendous responsibility—which takes time to develop. They are being asked to think critically, to solve problems, to create a lesson, and to present it to the class—processes that teachers sometimes find difficult to do, and that must therefore be painstakingly developed in youngsters. Certainly the effort is well worth the result and deserves encouragement at all grade levels, regardless of the discipline being taught.

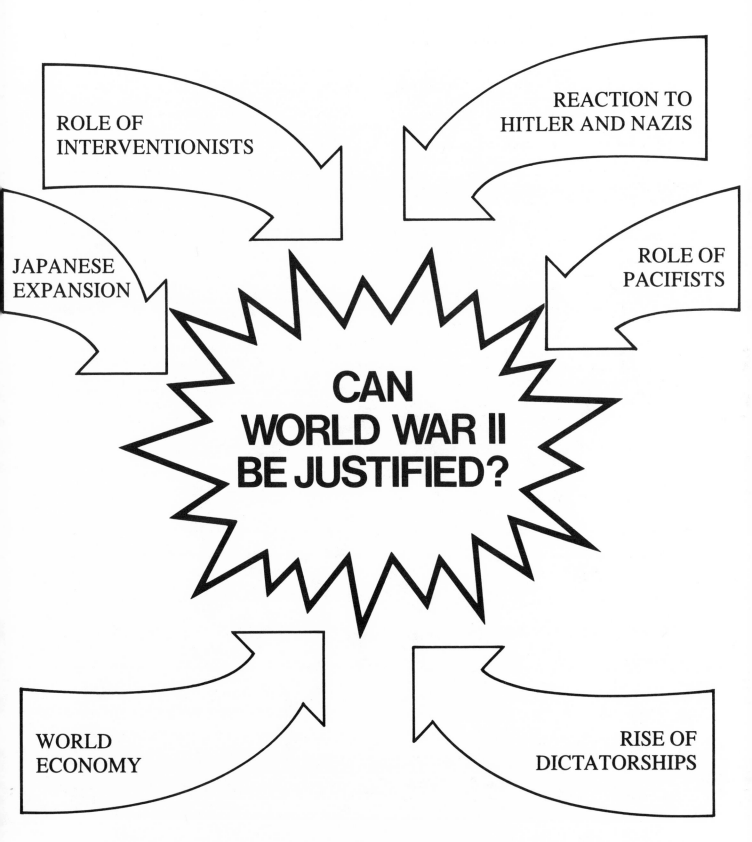

ROLE OF INTERVENTIONISTS

REACTION TO HITLER AND NAZIS

JAPANESE EXPANSION

ROLE OF PACIFISTS

CAN WORLD WAR II BE JUSTIFIED?

WORLD ECONOMY

RISE OF DICTATORSHIPS

GROUP WORK INFORMATION SHEET

Topic _____   Group Number _____

                                      Group Grade _____

I.   **Group Members**

    A.   **Leader:**

    B.   **Others**

        1.

        2.

        3.

        4.

II. **Questions/Subtopics**

    A.

    B.

    C.

    D.

III. **Activities**

List and explain in detail the specific activities your group will use to share your information with the rest of the class.

IV. **Time Estimate**

Approximately how much time will your group need to complete your activities? _____

GROUP WORK PROJECT IDEAS

When working on your group projects, it may sometimes be difficult to come up with ideas for the activities section of your "Group Work Information Sheet." The following list represents some suggestions that may aid you in planning a presentation. Keep in mind that a good presentation has several activities. Add any ideas of your own to the list.

1. Maps, graphs, charts
2. Oral presentations
3. Audiotape cassettes
4. Videotapes
5. Slide presentations
6. Overhead and opaque projections
7. Political cartoons, posters, drawings, paintings
8. Poetry, readings, quotes
9. Simulations and role-playing situations
10. Polls, surveys, questionnaires
11. Games
12. Debates, panel discussions
13. Bulletin board displays
14. News reports
15. Interviews
16. Projects, dioramas, scale models
17. Questioning techniques
18. Collages
19. Displays

ACTIVITIES FOR U.S. POLICY IN HAWAII

1. An oral report on the annexation of Hawaii

2. A map showing the distance between Hawaii and the continental United States

3. An oral report on how the United States first became involved in Hawaii

4. Political cartoons about the Monroe Doctrine, isolationism, and expansionism

5. A taped discussion about isolationism and expansionism

6. A calligraphy description of the Monroe Doctrine

7. A time line showing changes in the U.S. national interest in the late 1800's

8. A debate on whether to annex Hawaii

9. A time line showing U.S. involvement in Hawaii

10. A puppet show on the Hawaiian Revolution

11. A slide presentation on the Hawaiian Revolution

12. Webster cards on isolationism and expansionism

ACTIVITIES FOR
THE SPANISH-AMERICAN WAR

1. A taped report telling why the war was fought

2. A picture summary of Evangelina Cisneros and the role she played in the war

3. A dittoed example of "Yellow Journalism"

4. A poem on why the *Maine* was blown up

5. A map showing U.S. possessions after the Spanish-American War

6. A political cartoon about why the Spanish-American War was called a "splendid little war"

7. An oral report on the Spanish-American War

8. A slide show on the Spanish-American War

9. A political cartoon about why the Spanish-American War was so short

10. A map of Cuba, highlighting the charge up San Juan Hill

11. A political cartoon of Admiral Dewey and his role in the war

12. A poem describing the problems faced by Evangelina Cisneros

13. A role play about a reaction to the blowing up of the *Maine*

14. A time line showing important events in the war

15. A map of the world showing places where important battles were fought

16. A letter to the publishers of the text inquiring about the source of their information about Evangelina Cisneros

17. A play

18. A drawing of a battleship

19. A newscast on the war

20. An opaque projector presentation of maps

EVALUATION CHECKLIST

Group Leader _____

Group Objectives

1.

2.

3.

Group Activities

1.

2.

3.

Checklist	Yes	No
1. Were the objectives realistic?	_____	_____
2. Were the activities selected appropriate to the objectives?	_____	_____
3. Did the group meet its objectives?	_____	_____
4. Did the group members feel they met their objectives?	_____	_____
5. Did the group members work well together?	_____	_____
6. Did the group explore varied resources?	_____	_____
7. Were there enough resources?	_____	_____

Comments

STUDENT EVALUATION
OF PERFORMANCE

Circle the number that is most appropriate (1 is the lowest and 5 is the highest).

1. **The student was loud and clear.**

    1   2   3   4   5

2. **The student showed poise.**

    1   2   3   4   5

3. **The student's presentation was interesting and used a variety of techniques.**

    1   2   3   4   5

4. **The student's coverage of the topic was informative and complete.**

    1   2   3   4   5

5. **The student's presentation was well organized and smooth.**

    1   2   3   4   5

6. **What letter grade would you give to this presentation? (Circle your answer.)**

    A+   A   A−   B+   B   B−   C+   C   C−   D+   D   D−   F

Comments

PART II

Guide to Activities

Activities to Increase Student Participation

MINICOURSES

Teaching a minicourse is an idea whose time has come. These offerings serve both teachers and students. They allow teachers to experiment with methods they might not feel comfortable with in a regular classroom setting. And they allow students to explore a variety of interests in a short period of time.

If a school does not have minicourses, one way to start is for the teacher to get a small group of students together and try out an idea—one day a week after school or during a study hall.

I teach a minicourse entitled "Cosmos." A list of activities created by students in the class follows. This list represents an application of the model discussed in Part I. Following that is a minicourse poll and its results, an example of some of the ideas carried out by one student. Then there is a description of the minicourses taught in our school. They may help other teachers generate interest in minicourses in their schools.

Cosmos

TOPIC: Life in Outer Space

1. Is there life in outer space?
2. Are there UFO's?
3. Have we been visited by forms of alien life?
4. How far might alien life be from earth?
5. What might living things from other planets look like?
6. How would such living things communicate?

ACTIVITIES

1. Drawings of possible UFO's and forms of alien life
2. Oral report on UFO's and possible sightings
3. Videotape interview discussing UFO's
4. Play
5. Maps of major sightings
6. Graphs or charts indicating planets or systems with possible life
7. Debate: Are UFO's for real?
8. Cartoons on forms of alien life
9. Bulletin board with articles
10. Student opinion poll

Minicourse Poll

NAME: _____

1. Do you think the space program is worthwhile? (Circle one.)

   Yes   No

   Explain why you said yes or no.

   _____

   _____

   _____

   _____

   _____

   _____

   _____

2. List the following issues from most important to least important: controlling the economy, alternate power sources, the space program, developing more nuclear weapons.

   a. _____

   b. _____

   c. _____

   d. _____

Minicourse Poll Results

1. Percentage of those who said yes to the question "Do you think the space program is worthwhile?" 90%

2. Percentage of those who said no to the same question. 10%

3. Percentage of those who said that the #1 issue was:

   a. Controlling the economy   78%
   b. The space program   2%
   c. Finding alternative power   15%
   d. Nuclear weapons   5%

4. Some of the best answers of those who responded affirmatively to the question "Do you think the space program is worthwhile?"

   a. So we can learn more about the things around us.
   b. Because we could really find out if someone out there is alive.
   c. By exploring space and other planets, some day we may be able to live on other planets or find out if other civilizations are out there.
   d. Because if there is a planet like Earth with people living on it, it would be worthwhile to find out.
   e. For every dollar spent in the space program, five are returned to the economy in new technology.
   f. To know the mysteries of space.

Minicourse Descriptions

WOODCRAFT

Students will produce, on an individual basis, sculptures made from tree branches and logs, which they supply. They will also make wood and plastic jewelry. This minicourse was formed to explore areas not usually found in the normal Industrial Arts program. Therefore, no Industrial Arts shop projects will be constructed. The course invites both boys and girls to develop a knowledge of handtools, woodworking skills, and an appreciation of the craftsperson.

GIRLS' SPORTS

This democratically organized minicourse will adapt to fit the group of girls participating. A few of the activities it includes are paddle tennis, gymnastics, volleyball, tumbling, and dancing. If you are sportsminded, you probably would like to try the Sports Minicourse.

BOYS' SPORTS

This minicourse emphasizes team sports, such as baseball, basketball, football, hockey. One cycle may be spent on learning and playing ping-pong. Any boy who is interested in playing sports and being a sport is invited to join.

ELECTRONICS

This minicourse gives students a chance to construct various projects—an electronic organ, a metronome, an AM transmitter, etc.—from reusable kits. It is *not* open to anyone who took it last year.

POP MUSIC

Students in this group will sing popular and semipopular songs. Based on the ability of the members of the group, there will also be part singing.

EXPLORING UNSOLVED MYSTERIES

Students will read and discuss some of the world's greatest unsolved mysteries and phenomena: The Mystery of the Lost Continent of Atlantis, The Legend of Bigfoot, The Lost Patrol That Vanished in the Bermuda Triangle, and more. This minicourse is *not* open to students who have taken it before.

FRENCH

This minicourse introduces conversational French with the use of the Systems 80 machine. It also includes some culture and history.

CALCULATOR

This minicourse gives the opportunity to learn the proper way to use the calculator. Some calculators may be provided, but students should try to bring their own.

FUN WITH MATH

Games, puzzles, and magic squares will show interested students fun uses of math.

CERAMICS

Students in this minicourse will create functional and nonfunctional art objects from clay.

PAINTING

Students in this minicourse will work with watercolor, acrylic, and tempera paint.

SCIENCE FICTION

What is science fiction? Are science fiction authors simply imaginative dreamers writing fairy tales? Or are they scientists offering us a glimpse of the future?

This minicourse will attempt to answer these questions and others on this misunderstood topic. In addition, the group will participate in reading short stories and novels.

CROSS-COUNTRY

One part, for cross-country runners, is an outdoor sports run during the fall season. Class members will run some very basic workouts and compete against each other in actual races.

In another part, a spring sport, students will take part in runs of various lengths on the track. In addition, there will be some field events, such as the long jump and the high jump. Only those with a real desire to find out what running is all about should sign up.

ADVERTISING
This minicourse explores the methods used in advertising. Students will create and enact on videotape advertisements trying to sell a product.

COMMUNICATION THROUGH MUSIC
In this course students will listen to music that develops a theme. Each student will (1) develop a program that communicates a message through a series of songs and (2) interpret the themes of other students.

ANIMALS
This course is designed to develop humane attitudes toward all animals and the environments in which they live. Topics to be discussed include animal care, endangered animals, and wildlife conservation.

PHOTOGRAPHY
This course is designed for the beginning photographer. It includes a variety of topics, such as how to handle a camera, parts of the camera, lighting techniques. Students will also be able to develop their own prints. *10 students only.*

EXERCISE FOR HEALTH
Learn all about eating right, exercising to stay in shape, and how to diet properly. Come and exercise your way to health.

SAND TERRARIUMS
You need not be an artist to create a beautiful sand terrarium. The techniques of layering, mounding, and shaping are simple and easy to learn. Students provide their own supplies and materials.

EASY-TO-MAKE HOLIDAY GIFTS
Students will create simple but attractive items suitable for holiday gifts, using materials brought from home. Participants must be prepared to bring materials needed for their chosen project. *10 students only.*

WRITING YOUR OWN BOOK
You can become the author of a book that looks professionally bound. Once you learn this simple process, you can create attractive books to keep or use as gifts. Students are expected to provide some simple supplies.

BRASS ENSEMBLE
This minicourse is open to all students who play a brass instrument. It provides an opportunity to play these instruments in small groups.

PERCUSSION ENSEMBLE
This course is open to all students who have played drums for at least one year. It is an opportunity to play music for drums only.

COSMOS
This minicourse examines the many mysteries of the universe. The planets, the stars, and the place of humans in the cosmos are its main focus of study.

LEATHERCRAFT
This minicourse introduces students to leatherwork. Students will complete simple leather projects. *7th graders only.*

ANIMATED FILMMAKING
This minicourse introduces students to animated filmmaking. Students will create and produce a film based on their own ideas. *12 students only.*

CURRENT EVENTS

How to make the study of current events come alive in the classroom has long been a difficult task for many teachers. Far too often this is done by simply having students bring in news stories to discuss. While such an activity has its place under limited conditions, it should be just one of many techniques used. The following is a collection of strategies I have created to deal with the study of current events.

The first strategy concerns the creation of a news team. All students become involved by collecting, sorting, and writing stories. I use this technique on a monthly basis. First I have students form groups. Then I ask for a volunteer group to be responsible for doing an in-depth study of current events for one month. During the month I give these students class time in the library for their project. At month's end they must perform their newscast for the rest of the class. The following month a new group takes over. This procedure continues until all groups have performed and then we repeat the process. No two broadcasts are the same.

Students are encouraged to be as creative as possible. Many groups have "dressed up" for the occasion; made fake microphones; created a backdrop with a news team logo; used maps, charts, and graphs; interviewed various school personnel and other subjects. As teacher, it has often been my job to try to keep students within the realm of possibility. This can be a formidable task. One group surprised me, however, by phoning and inviting the town mayor for an interview. He accepted, and that newscast served to be a learning experience for those students, which they will remember for the rest of their lives.

The remaining activities in this section—"In the News," "Issues and Answers," and "Face the Students"—are self-explanatory. They may be used on a regular basis, or on a limited basis, as extension/enrichment exercises.

Current Events Newscast

I. General Instructions

    A. Include stories of major interest on the following levels in your presentation:

        1. International
        2. National
        3. State
        4. Local
        5. School

    B. Use newspapers, TV, magazines, etc., as sources for your stories.

    C. Make interviews an important part of your presentation.

    D. Keep stories short and write them in an interesting and informative way.

    E. Give reports on special topics (such as inflation, energy, the space program) as a part of your presentation.

    F. Include an editorial—an expression of personal opinion on a topic—at the end of your program.

    G. Watch TV news shows for ideas for setting up your program.

    H. Plan your newscast to run about 15 to 30 minutes.

II. Grading Procedure

You will be graded on—

    A. Length of program.

    B. How well stories were reported.

    C. Types of stories reported—coverage of all areas.

    D. Overall structure of program.

    E. Quality of written stories.

III. Sample Program Structure
(You may develop your own.)

    A. Introduction

    B. International News

    C. National News

    D. State News

    E. Local News

    F. School News

    G. Special Story

    H. Editorial

    I. Windup

IV. Further Information

    A. Write notes for your stories on *one* side of the paper.

    B. Shorten stories to *no more than* three paragraphs.

    C. Try to break up monotony in your presentation with a "news flash" or commercial.

    D. If you plan to use props (such as background pictures and maps, telephones, typewriters), make them at home or bring them from home.

    E. Newscasters can "dress up" for authenticity.

    F. On-the-spot reporting can take place in the halls or classrooms.

    G. Time will be given for—

        1. Collecting stories.
        2. Sorting stories—select only those you wish to use.
        3. Rewriting stories.
        4. Planning and writing a script.
        5. Taping the show. (You may videotape the broadcast if you have the facilities.)

"In the News"

    I. Create a two-minute newsclip about an event of current interest in the school or community.

    II. Research the topic, interview the necessary people, and prepare a script in the style of CBS's "In the News."

    III. Videotape the newsclip.

    IV. Suggested topics may include the following:

        A. Activities generated by the PTA

        B. Community issues gleaned from the local newspaper

        C. Updates on local sports teams

        D. Program considerations of the Board of Education, such as the district program for the gifted and talented

"Issues and Answers"

Organize a debate on such school issues as the following:

    1. Cafeteria food
    2. Coeducational sports teams
    3. Honor codes

4. Study halls
5. Dress codes
6. Gum chewing
7. Grades
8. Hall procedure
9. Value of the library
10. Other

Videotape the debate as it might appear on ABC's ''Issues and Answers.''

''Face the Students''

Whom would you like to invite to school for an interview? Select someone of particular interest to your students and send an invitation. If the person accepts the invitation, she or he would come to class for an interview by a select panel of students. Students should prepare their questions beforehand and the teacher should check them prior to the interview.

Some suggestions for possible subjects to interview are as follows:

1. Local school personnel
2. Student council representatives
3. Teachers
4. An interesting local resident
5. The mayor and council members
6. State legislators
7. The governor
8. The President of the United States*
9. Members of Congress
10. Sports and entertainment personalities.**

VOCABULARY

No subject can be sensibly approached without an understanding of the key vocabulary terms of the topic being studied. For example, how can students be expected to study the effects of propaganda on our society unless and until they know the meaning of propaganda?
Two techniques that I have used follow. One concerns an understanding of how to use a particular word in a sentence and is self-explanatory. The other is more difficult. It is called a ''Vocabulary Idea Sheet'' because it does a good deal more than give a definition. The pro-

cess was adapted from *Word Power Made Easy* (9). (An excellent personal resource also.)

The ''Vocabulary Idea Sheet'' contains all the necessary items for helping students understand often difficult words. Begin by having students gather in small groups. Each group is then assigned a word and provided with a dictionary, a thesaurus, the text, and, most importantly, instructions.

The instructions are simple. Tell students they are going to create an idea about a particular word rather than just find a definition. To begin, they must create a short definition of the word. This can come from the more detailed, formal definition usually found in the dictionary, popular songs of the day, or even a short, catchy phrase they might have heard around the house. They may also use a thesaurus. Whatever they decide upon must capture the essence of the word.

Then students follow the short definition with three items: (1) a more formal definition, (2) the word used properly in a complex sentence, and (3) a personal experience expressing the meaning of the word to which students can relate. Finally, they spell out the word.

The formal definition is the standard kind found in a dictionary, glossary, or text. Students must precede the definition with ''This word refers to . . .'' or ''This word means . . .'' The use of the word in a sentence should indicate an understanding of its meaning. Sentences may be culled from the dictionary, the text, or the students' own imagination. The real creativity comes from the personal experience. Here, the student must apply the word, or at least its meaning, to a circumstance that has direct significance to him or her. Situations at home, play, or school usually provide many choices.

During this activity the teacher can circulate throughout the class to assist wherever necessary, and when a group has finished, check its work for spelling and grammatical errors. Group members then write what they have created on the chalkboard in the following schema:

1. Short definition
2. Formal definition
3. Word used in sentence
4. Personal experience.

By the end of the class all students should have copied into their notes the results of the activity.

The ''Vocabulary Idea Sheet'' that follows contains examples of student work.

---

*You never know unless you try. We sent a letter to former President Richard Nixon, a New Jersey resident. Although he could not accept, he did respond to our invitation.

**We have also received responses from such people as Richard Pryor, David Spielberg, and George Burns. We were fortunate to interview Willard Scott of NBC's ''Today'' show.

Using Words in a Sentence

SMALL GROUP EXERCISE

1. Each group selects a new vocabulary word.
2. Group members construct a sentence using the word.
3. One member from each group writes the sentence on the board.
4. The entire class reviews the sentences.
5. Students write the final sentences in their notebooks.

Vocabulary Idea Sheet

1. *Prove it*
   This word means to show that something is just or right; in other words, to give a good reason for your actions. If a government fails to *justify* its going to war, it might lose the support of its people. You probably have to justify your coming in at 8:35 when you were told to be in at 8:30.

   JUSTIFY

2. *I hate war*
   This word refers to a person who is against all wars and favors settling all disputes between nations by peaceful means. During times of war, the *pacifist* might have refused to serve in the armed forces or might have served in a noncombat situation. Next time your parents want to physically punish you for something you did, say to them, ''Isn't it better to be a pacifist?''

   PACIFIST

3. *The tyrant*
   This word refers to a person exercising absolute authority, whose power is not limited either by law or the acts of any official body. Adolf Hitler was an excellent example of a *dictator*. We don't have this type of ruler in America because of the value we place on individual freedom.

   DICTATOR

4. *''Stuck in the middle again''*
   This line, from a popular song, refers to the vocabulary word that means *not* to go one way or the other; in other words, to be on neither side. The country of Sweden was *neutral* during World Wars I and II. You might find it hard to remain totally neutral during the argument or fight of a friend.

   NEUTRAL

5. *Friend*
   This word refers to those joined together for a common cause. The United States joined hands and became *allies* with other countries of the world to oppose the Axis powers of World War II. You might become allies with other members of your class to oppose the class bully.

   ALLY

6. *To plan ahead*
   This word refers to anything that is planned beforehand. President Roosevelt used the word *premeditate* in his speech to Congress when describing Japan's attack on Pearl Harbor. You should do this before going on a trip or taking a test.

   PREMEDITATE

ROLE PLAYING

Students enjoy acting in plays and situations. Ask one why he or she did not do homework and you will see an academy-award-winning performance. The lesson that follows is one I devised after watching the television movie *The Well*. In this role-playing activity, as in others, it is important to remember that the results will be different with different groups of students, because it relies on creative dialogue by students.

Be sure to allow one full period for the role play itself. Begin with a vocabulary lesson on the day before to familiarize students with the general concepts involved in the following words: *prejudice, racism, discrimination, radical,* and *conservative.*

On the day of the role play, distribute to each student a copy of the background information that is given in the lesson plan that follows. When everyone understands the situation, assign the roles. It is a good idea to assign the most vocal students to the panel. Teachers who know their students well can increase the chances for a successful lesson by typecasting them. Once students have read the descriptions of their roles and have had all their questions answered, the action begins.

The dialogue is purely creative. When all students are aware of the situation, they react according to the dictates of their roles. The role of the teacher in the exercise and in the evaluative followup is clearly stated.

One advantage of such lessons is that they can be created from many situations with a minimal amount of teacher planning, regardless of the course being taught.

Lesson Plan on Prejudice and Racism

I. Description

   This lesson uses the movie *The Well* as the basis for a role-playing exercise.

II. Background Information

   The scene is a quiet town that is predominantly white but with a sizable Black population. Race relations have never been perfect but they have been better than in most areas. There have been no serious outbursts of hatred on either side.

One day, a six year-old white girl disappeared. She was last seen playing in an open field near the highway by passing motorists. Also seen in the vicinity was a Black man, hitchhiking. The girl's parents reported her missing and the police picked up the Black man about a mile or so out of town. Members of the community are outraged. The girl has now been missing for eight hours. Tensions are high and some people want to storm the jail.

Community leaders call a meeting . . .

III. Characters

A. Panel (seated at a table in front of the class)

1. *Mayor.* You are in charge of the meeting. Your job is to maintain order and guide this group toward seeking a solution to the problem of community relations.

2.. *Police Chief.* You have come under criticism lately from Blacks and whites. Both groups have accused you of not doing enough for their side. How do you react to the current problem?

3. *Principal of High School.* Be able to give a picture of the poor race relations between students as a result of this problem. What do you suggest as a solution?

4. *Black Community Leader (Conservative).* You despise violence and work hard trying to improve community race relations. What suggestions do you have?

5. *White Community Leader (Conservative).* You despise violence and work hard trying to improve community race relations. What suggestions do you have?

B. Audience

1. *Radical Blacks.* You think there are whites in town who first hate Blacks and therefore want to harm the prisoner, simply because he is Black. Convince them that you will react violently if any harm comes to the prisoner.

2. *Radical Whites.* You believe that the Black man is guilty and the police are doing nothing to bring him to justice. Express your anger about this and tell what you might do to take justice into your own hands.

3. *Conservative Blacks.* Same as community leader on panel.

4. *Conservative Whites.* Same as community leader on panel.

5. *Mother of Girl.* You have nothing against Blacks but your husband is very prejudiced. You are extremely upset that your daughter is missing. What kind of plea do you make to the mayor and panel?

6. *Father of Girl.* You are very upset. You are not fond of Blacks and you want something done with the prisoner. What do you say to the mayor and police chief to convince them that you mean business?

C. Town Clerk

The teacher acts as town clerk. The clerk's job is to deliver the following messages several minutes apart to the mayor to read aloud:

1. A doll was found in a field near the road where the Black was hitchhiking.

2. A group of whites just beat up a Black, downtown. .

3. A group of Blacks just beat up a white, downtown.

4. The high school has just been vandalized.

5. The girl has now been missing for 12 hours. Mr. Mayor, ask for possible solutions to the problem.

6. *LAST MESSAGE*: The girl has just been found in an old abandoned well. She fell in by accident and is all right.

IV. Evaluation

A. Discussion (oral)

1. How do you define prejudice?

2. Why are people prejudiced?

3. Why do people jump to conclusions?

4. How do you think you fit your role?

5. Can we overcome prejudice?

B. Written (two paragraphs per question)

1. Express your feelings during the activity; concentrate on the role you played.

2. What do you think you have learned from this exercise?

GAMES

Don't be frightened by the word "game." Effectively used, games can be of enormous value in stimulating the hard-to-motivate as well as in providing an enjoyable change of pace for average and above-average students. There are many games on the market, ranging from the simple to the complex. A careful evaluation of the manufacturers' promotional material should help teachers determine their specific needs.

Some games, commonly seen on television, can be easily adapted for classroom use. For example, many teachers have developed their own interpretations of the well-known TV game "Jeopardy." The outline that follows is an adaptation I made for my classes. It is one of the most popular activities of the year. Teachers who wish to do so may use this version as a guide, changing whatever aspects they deem necessary.

Another game I use is "Junior College Bowl," an adaptation of TV's "College Bowl." An outline of this also is included.

A third game is one in which students write their personal reactions to a film, an activity they enjoy. While this technique may not be usable with all films, it can be most effective with certain ones. I simply tell my students that they are going to watch a film as critics. However, they must do more than describe what they saw and what they thought of the production; they must also write what they think the film was about. This last paragraph is the most important part of their critique.

This section includes a collection of student reactions to *Powers of Ten*, a Pyramid film that explores the relative distance between objects in the cosmos. Its starting point is the hand of a man in a park in Chicago. Through special effects the camera then retreats by powers of ten to the edge of the known universe, passing whole galaxies as it does so. Then it comes hurtling back to earth and explores the inner space of the man's hand by negative powers of ten. The reactions to this highly creative film represent some intuitive, divergent thinking by a group of average eighth grade students.

Finally, this section contains a strategy I devised for getting the best results possible when using films and filmstrips. It, too, was spawned from a popular TV game show. Many teachers express concern over the use of audiovisual materials because of disappointing student reactions. This "new approach," first published in the May, 1981, edition of *NJEA Review,* should allay such concerns.

"Jeopardy"

PREPARATION

Prepare for the game two days before playing it by telling students that they are going to play "Jeopardy" and outlining the material it will cover. Students prepare for the game by studying the material.

On the day of the game at the beginning of the period, draw the game board on the chalkboard (see attached). It is divided into five categories. Each category represents some aspect of the material that students have studied, and is followed by a list of points ranging from 10 to 50. Use five index cards, one for each category, and write five questions with amounts ranging from 10 to 50 points on each card, basing the amount on the difficulty of the question.

Divide the class into two teams—for example, boys against girls, for a very competitive atmosphere, or one half of the room against the other. Then write the names of each team on the board and explain the rules of play.

RULES OF PLAY

1. The teacher calls out a category and an amount—for example, "Important People" for 10 points.

2. The first person on either team to raise his/her hand can answer the question.

3. For a correct answer, the team gains 10 points; for an incorrect answer, the team loses 10 points. (My class does not go below zero into minus numbers.)

4. If the first answer is incorrect, the other team has an opportunity to answer the question. The same rules apply. If the second team chooses not to answer the question, play resumes as before.

5. After each response, the teacher records the appropriate score and crosses out the amount in the appropriate space on the game board.

6. Play continues until all questions have been used.

7. At this point the game goes into final jeopardy. The members of each team collaborate to select one member as their representative and to decide the amount of their accumulated points they wish to wager. They may wager all or a part of their holdings.

8. The two players chosen to represent their teams sit at the head of the class.

9. These two contestants receive a small piece of paper on which to write their team name and the number of points they wish to wager. (They cannot make any changes after the question is read.)

10. These contestants are given a final jeopardy question to which only they may respond. They write their answers on the paper, which the teacher collects after a minute or two.

11. The teacher first records the wagers under the teams' points and then reads each answer and states whether it is correct.

12. The winning team is awarded two points on its next test as an incentive to prepare for the next game.

Sample "JEOPARDY" Game Board

(This game board can be used in any discipline simply by changing categories and making up appropriate questions.)

IMPORTANT PEOPLE	VOCABULARY	DATES	WORLD WAR I	WORLD WAR II
10	10	10	10	10
20	20	20	20	20
30	30	30	30	30
40	40	40	40	40
50	50	50	50	50

Junior College Bowl

THE PURPOSE

1. This game serves as an effective review for a test or quiz.

2. It gives some of the above-average students a chance to use their talents.

3. It gives other students an opportunity to develop such skills as determining the main idea of material and composing penetrating questions.

4. This technique can be used with slower students if they are held responsible for smaller bits of information.

THE PLAY

1. Select three students to be responsible for knowing a particular section of information.

2. The rest of the class is responsible for writing and asking questions on the section.

3. No questions should require yes/no or either/or-type answers.

4. Students divide the questions into three groups according to difficulty (5 points, 10 points, 20 points) and submit them to the teacher one full day before the game.

5. There must be five questions per category.

6. The teacher quickly checks the questions before the game to make sure they are properly categorized.

7. On the day of the game students' questions are returned so that each one can ask his/her questions.

8. Use a specific time limit for answering questions from each category.

9. Students ask questions one at a time in succession. They start with those in the easiest category, and ask all of them before going on to the next category. If a player misses a question, no points are deducted and the question passes to the next contestant.

10. Players raise their hands to answer. The teacher may wish to prompt those who need encouragement, to ensure their participation.

11. For authenticity, have students make name cards and point cards to flip over when the time limit is up. A timer with a bell will also add to the excitement.

12. Points awarded are based on the value of the question.

13. The award consists of a ''Special Awards'' certificate to keep on file and 2 points added to the winner's test.

SPECIAL NOTE: Keep track of each class winner for a playoff at the end of the year. Then have a playoff among classes for a school winner. This person can receive a trophy or plaque and gain some local newspaper fame.

Student Reactions to Powers of Ten

1. I think the whole idea of the movie was to show you that there isn't any end to things. It also shows how much men have to learn. When they go out real far, there is still more out there that man hasn't learned yet. When they got real close to the guy's hand, they showed that there is still more for men to learn on Earth. It also showed that there is an infinity to knowledge that men can learn on Earth and beyond.

2. I think I get the idea but I don't know how to say it. The closest I could come is that from the smallest particle to the infinity of the universe, everything is connected or part of a single unit just separated by a distance of a few inches or a million miles, but it's still all part of the universe and how you see it depends on where you are or your perspective.

3. I think the movie was trying to show us space, earth, and the human body in a very short period of time. I think this trip was also saying that space, earth, and the human body are all related and are all joined. When we entered the human hand, we ended right back in something like space . . . Every minute took you a step farther to seek different places.

4. Even though we think we are big and influential, this film showed us that we are such a small part of space and we are even a very small part of the world here on earth. Compared to everything else in the world and universe, we are almost nothing.

5. I think the idea of showing the darkness of space and then the darkness into the human hand was a way of saying we may be made up of something from space, or characteristics of mass are the same.

Films and Filmstrips: A New Approach*

The lights go out and it suddenly becomes dark and quiet. The time doesn't matter. It could be 9:00 a.m. It could be 1:00 p.m. It might be a cloudy day, a sunny day, or the brink of a winter blizzard. It's filmstrip time, or movie time, and that which should amount to an exciting break from the routine soon takes on the appearance of a slumber party.

As we look out over their somewhat less-than-enthusiastic faces, it becomes painfully clear to us that films, filmstrips, and the like make for a bit dry, if not downright boring, class period.

Should it be? No! We all have, or should have, painstakingly gone through the tedious chore of ordering, previewing, comparing films and filmstrips to select "the best that money can buy." We are always convincing ourselves that it "is" good and they "are" going to like it. Why, then, do we consistently bear witness to a mass "tuning out" by our students during a lesson like this?

The answer to this question does not lie in the direction of the clock, the weather, or the color tie we happen to be wearing that day. Instead, we must think in terms of what we are doing or not doing to make it interesting.

We are all aware of the effect too much unrestricted television has had and continues to have on all of us. Studies will undoubtedly be done for years to come on this topic, but suffice it to say that many in today's society have long surpassed their saturation point in dealing effectively with video material. The on-off switch of our television set allows us to turn off, tune out, or otherwise forget the world around us and escape into a realm of do-nothingness. Is it then so surprising to see a group of students react in what we view as a negative way to our well-chosen film or filmstrip? No. But it is a situation which can be rectified.

An alternative I would like to offer concerns a game. The game is designed for maximum participation. Everyone gets involved—including the hard-to-motivate. I call it "Classmate Feud." The name is unimportant; the results are what count.

The rules of the game are simple. You begin with an explanation of the rules to the class just prior to viewing a film or filmstrip. As the material is being shown, all students in the class must copy down anywhere from three to five questions that they plan to use in questioning the teams. It would be a good idea to encourage the acquisition of as many questions as possible but even the slower students manage to get three. They also must have the answers to the questions in order to validate a contestant's response.

After viewing the material, ask for volunteers to participate on one of two teams. Each team should consist of three members of varied ability. Try to have a more advanced student, an average student, and perhaps a slower student, who you think would not be overly embarrassed, on each team. Teams can be designated by letter, such as Team A vs. Team B; number; or special name, such as the Blue Team vs. the Yellow Team. A scorekeeper is needed and the teacher should act as moderator and judge, to determine the validity of questions asked. The game is now ready to begin.

By raising his/her hand, a student is chosen to begin the game by asking Team A a question. The three members of the team are allowed to confer with each other for five seconds before giving an answer. They should designate one member of their team to be the spokesman to give the agreed-upon reply. Should Team A give a correct answer, they receive a point. Should they give a wrong answer, Team B will receive the option of accepting or rejecting the same question. If they accept and are correct, they receive a point and a "bonus" question asked by another student. If they accept and are wrong, they do not receive a bonus question and play returns to Team A. If they do not accept the question missed by Team A, they receive a totally new question asked by another student and the same rules apply.

The game is over when the time prescribed by the teacher is up. It is wise to set a time limit for the game so there will be no dispute as to which team is the victor. It is also wise for the teacher to have a few questions on hand in case of need for a tie-breaker.

I think you will find this game useful. It is certainly effective. And the next time you decide to show a movie or filmstrip in your class, take notice. The catnaps and overriding sense of boredom will soon disappear as students busy themselves with copying down questions and answers. And for the first time in a long time, during a lesson such as this, you will find them "all" paying attention.

*NJEA Review 54, no. 9 (May 1981), p. 25. Reprinted with permission.

PROJECTS FAIR

Students enjoy doing projects. Such activities afford them the opportunity to assimilate information they have learned and present it creatively. Not all students may find it easy to work in this milieu, but with proper guidance even the most reluctant student will become enthusiastically involved.

Each year since the nation's bicentennial, I have been conducting a History Fair. Over the years, it has proved to be a valuable means of tapping a creative resource hitherto unnoticed in students. With careful planning, the fair has consistently been successful. Some of my students have gone on to participate in regional and state contests. One student, who won awards on both the regional and state levels, also competed in National History Day, a contest on the national level held in Washington, D.C.

What follows is a carefully mapped-out sequence of events designed to aid teachers in setting up a fair of their own. Keep in mind that these guidelines may be used for other kinds of fairs—science, art, or interdisciplinary. If the events are plotted on a calendar early in the year, a minimum of effort will reap great rewards.

Schedule of Events

I. Initial/Advance Planning

    A. Initial Plug
Discuss with students the idea of a projects fair. I expose my students to the idea of a history fair early in the year. Since our fair has been running for several years, I have a set of slides complete with script, which I show students to motivate them.

    B. Rules Sheet
Shortly after the initial plug, distribute and discuss the accompanying "Rules Sheet."

    C. Collecting Project Ideas
This part of the advance planning will help ensure that each student works on a worthwhile project. Set a date for each student to choose an idea for a project. (The cooperation of the school librarian at this point will be very helpful.) By that deadline students must submit to the teacher an index card giving their name and homeroom, the names of those with whom they will be working, their project title, and a brief description of how they plan to carry out their project. After reviewing these cards, I write "Approved" or "Not approved" on each one, explain that label, and return the cards. This is also a good opportunity to add any constructive comments and suggestions. No students should go ahead without advance approval. In this way the teacher can maintain control over the quality and diversity of the projects submitted. (Approved projects have included a model of Mt. Rushmore, a replica of the atom bomb, a gallery of inventions through time, a scale model of a local church, colonial dolls.) All approved project titles are then placed on a master list next to each student's name to facilitate checking projects and assigning grades.

    D. Letter to Parents/Guardians
If any students have not selected a project idea by the due date (and there are usually a few), send a letter home to their parents/guardians. The letter (which follows this outline) simply informs the parents/guardians of their child's failure to meet the first deadline.

    E. Setting the Date
Setting the date for the fair demands a bit of attention. First, check for a tentative date with the building principal, who is best qualified to note any conflicts with other school programs. It is also wise to check the town's social calendar. Competing with bingo games, bowling leagues, and spaghetti dinners can be devastating to fair attendance. A final check with the PTA to avoid interference with its schedule should help in firming up a date.

II. Three Weeks Before the Fair

    A. Notifying the Local Newspaper
Most local newspapers are willing to print an article about a school fair if they receive the information in time. This can be an opportunity for students to write for publication.

    B. Inviting Parents/Guardians
A letter containing the time, date, and place of the fair sent home to parents/guardians will give them the opportunity to plan ahead to attend. A sample follows.

    C. Inviting Special Guests
I keep a list of educators and others who have expressed an interest in this enterprise. It contains the names of people I have met at workshops and at regional and state fairs, the chairperson of our high school Social Studies Department, and the leaders of local senior citizens groups. Use the letter sent to parents/guardians.

    D. Securing Judges
Many faculty members may be willing to assist in judging the projects. The expertise of shop, art, and home economics teachers, for example, would be especially helpful. Be sure to arrange for their assistance well in advance.

E. Notifying School Staff
Members of the school staff, especially those who work with youngsters in self-contained classrooms, need to be apprised of key elements that directly affect them. While not every teacher of a self-contained classroom may embrace the concept of the fair, most will actively participate and have their students submit projects. Therefore, they need to know about—

1. *The location.* If the school gym is the best location for the fair, be sure to obtain permission from the physical education teachers. Or if another location is available, be sure to make arrangements in advance for its use.

2, *Setting up projects.* Ask the teachers themselves the most convenient time for their classes to set up their projects. Then make a schedule of these times and show it to the teachers for any final comments.

3. *Dismantling projects.* It would be wise at this point to let teachers know when projects are to be removed. More on this later.

4. *Securing tables.* Many teachers have tables in their classrooms, which, if not in use, they will probably lend for the fair. (Also consider using other equipment such as the risers used by the chorus.)

III. One Week Before the Fair

A. Reminding the Judges
Even the most altruistic people occasionally forget what they have volunteered to do. A short, polite reminder to the judges at this point will allay any fears that they may not show up for the judging.

B. Scheduling Project Setup and Dismantling
Make a schedule for student participants telling them exactly when and where to bring their projects on the day of the fair, and when to dismantle them. (Also see II.E. Notifying School Staff.) Such advance notice will mean a smoother operation for everyone.

C. Scheduling Visits
Setting up a schedule for individual classes to visit the fair will avoid overcrowding.

D. Securing Custodial Help
It is a good idea to arrange for the assistance of school custodians some time before the fair. One week should normally suffice, but if more time is necessary, by all means make these arrangements earlier.

E. Securing Awards
If you plan to identify winners with certificates (as I do), or with ribbons, be sure to have enough on hand. It is better to be generous than frugal—especially with "Honorable Mention" awards. (Each child who enters our fair receives a "Certificate of Participation" designed by our art teacher. This helps promote enthusiasm and maintain interest for the following year. I also have been fortunate to receive money from our Student Council to purchase trophies for our "Best in Fair" award winners.)

F. Dittoing State Fair Information
Since our "Best in Fair" award winners are sent on to the regional level of the state contest, copies of all pertinent information are dittoed to give to each student who qualifies.

IV. Day of the Fair

A. Setting Up
Plan to spend the day at the fair location where students bring in and set up their projects according to schedule. My principal has arranged that I may be in the gymnasium all day. Since I make it mandatory for students in all my classes to do a project, they meet me there at the scheduled time and spend the period setting up their projects.

1. Use morning announcements to remind students as they arrive at school to bring their projects to the site of the fair (up to one-half hour before the beginning of school in our case). Be sure to be on the spot to direct students where to leave their projects. Later in the day, according to plan, they can come back to set them up.

2. During the setting up, it is wise to have the following on hand:
   a. *Five or six strong students*—to carry tables from the classrooms to the fair site. This procedure should take about 20 minutes and should be done at the beginning of the first period.
   b. *Masking tape and marker*—to mark each table to know where to return it after the fair.
   c. *Schedule for class setup*—to remind teachers who forget to send their students to set up their projects.

B. Judging Projects
This process takes place after school. By that time, all projects should be set up, the site clear of students, and the judges ready to go to work. The following points should be helpful in this most difficult aspect of the fair:

1. Have a list of criteria for judging projects. This minimizes subjectivity and aids the judges greatly. (A copy of the criteria I use follows this outline.)

2. Judge projects according to grade level. A fifth grader should not be judged by the same criteria as an eighth grader.

3. After the judges decide individually what they feel are the top projects for each grade level, they should meet, discuss their choices, draw up a single revised list, and revisit those projects as a group. Projects that receive a majority vote are designated ''Best in Fair''; the remaining projects on the list receive ''Honorable Mention'' awards.

4. After the judging, go around and place the awards on each project.

C. History Fair Night
Most of the work is now over and it is time to welcome the guests. Our fair runs from 7:00 to 9:00 p.m. when parents, members of the community, and other invited guests view the projects. Some suggestions to consider for the evening are as follows:

1. Music playing over the public address system can help soothe irate parents who do not see an award next to their child's project.

2. A bulletin board display explaining the theme of the fair (if there is one), or a photographic display of past fairs (if there have been others), can be helpful to visitors.

V. Student Visitation Day

A. Visitation
The day after the night of the fair have students come in class groups to view the projects. For example, if seventh and eighth graders are departmentalized, have them come during their social studies periods. Reserve the last period of the day for cleaning up.

B. The Big Cleanup
After all students have an opportunity to view the projects, the cleanup procedure begins.

1. Since my classes meet in the gym all day, I have quite a few ''volunteers'' during the last period.

2. Ten minutes before the end of the period, fifth graders come to the gym to claim their projects. When these students have gone, the volunteers start returning empty tables.

3. Five minutes before the end of the period, sixth graders come to get their projects. Then their tables are returned.

4. When the bell rings to end the last period of the day, seventh and eighth graders come to retrieve their projects.

5. At this time, my homeroom class returns the rest of the tables, delivers any unclaimed projects to their owners, and sweeps the gym.

VI. After the Fair

A. Send a letter to the parents/guardians of students who did not submit a project. If students receive a grade for their efforts, this will inform their parents/guardians of their failure. (A copy of such a letter follows.)

B. Be sure the award winners are aware of all information concerning the next level of competition, should there be any.

C. If you plan to have a report of the fair published in the local newspaper, be sure to send out photographs and a press release early.

D. One of the most important tasks after the fair is to send thank-you notes. They take only a few minutes but they show people that their efforts have been appreciated. Among those to remember are the following:

1. Judges

2. Administrators

3. Secretaries

4. Those who gave a bit extra, such as the art teacher.

History Fair Rules Sheet

I. General Information

   A. The date

   B. The place
      (Gymnasium or other suitable place)

   C. Awards
      Winners will be designated by award certificates, have their pictures appear in the local newspaper, and receive a trophy.

   D. Categories
      1. Upper grades
         a. *The eighth grade.* The History Fair project is mandatory. Projects will be geared toward American history from the "Period of Exploration" to the present.
         b. *The seventh grade.* The choice of projects is at the discretion of the social studies teacher.
      2. Lower grades
         a. *The sixth grade.* The choice of projects is at the discretion of the individual teacher. Projects should be geared toward the social studies subject covered.
         b. *The fifth grade.* Once again the choice of projects is at the discretion of the individual teacher. Projects should be geared toward the social studies subject covered.

II. Specific Rules

   A. All projects must adhere to the theme of the fair (if there is one).

   B. *NO* toys or kits should be used.

   C. No baked goods, please.

   D. More than one person may work on a particular project, providing the teacher in charge agrees, and there is enough work for each student.

   E. Parents are encouraged to assist their children, but they should limit their aid to the selection of materials and constructive criticism. The project itself should be done by the student.

   F. Any models, dioramas, etc., should be made according to scale, using the knowledge the student has gained in shop and mechanical drawing classes.

   G. Projects are just that—*PROJECTS*. Art work and reports should accompany, not substitute for, a project.

   H. Each project must be accompanied by a brief, legibly written or typewritten paper containing the following:
      1. One or more paragraphs on the historical relevance of the project, showing the impact the subject has had, or continues to have, on society, and indicating the research done.
      2. A description of the construction of the project—including how it was put together and what materials and procedures were used.
      3. A bibliography giving at least two sources other than the text and an encyclopedia.

LETTER TO PARENTS/GUARDIANS
OF STUDENTS WHO HAVE NOT MET
PROJECT DEADLINE

Dear (Parent/Guardian):

Our annual History Fair will be approaching soon. It will be held _____. All students were asked to select a project by _____ so that they would have plenty of time to work on it. All students will receive a grade for their project, which will represent a substantial part of the third marking period grade. Your son/daughter _____ has not yet chosen a project and there is not much time left.

Sincerely,

Jim Kelly
Social Studies Teacher

Please sign and return to school.

_____
Parent/Guardian Signature

INVITATION TO PARENTS/GUARDIANS AND SPECIAL GUESTS

Dear (Parent/Guardian/Special Guest):

I would like to take this opportunity to invite you and your family to our annual History Fair. The Richard Butler History Fair, begun in 1976, has become an annual event looked forward to by students and community members alike. It continues to provide students the opportunity to tap their creativity and sharpen necessary skills.

"Best in Fair" award winners will be able to participate in the regional contest at _____ on _____. Winners there will go on to compete on the state level, hoping to enter national competition in June.

Our fair will be held in the Richard Butler School gymnasium, Thursday, March 11, from 7:00 to 9:00 p.m.

Come join us for an enjoyable evening and see what our children can accomplish.

Very truly yours,

Jim Kelly
Social Studies Teacher

LETTER TO PARENTS/GUARDIANS OF STUDENTS WHO DID NOT DO PROJECT

To the Parent/Guardian of _____:

On _____, the Richard Butler School held its_____ annual history fair. Your child was expected to do a project. Enough time was given to select an idea, research the idea, and do the project. Your child chose not to do this.

As this project represents a substantial part of the third marking period grade, your child stands a very good chance of failing for this marking period.

Please sign and return this entire sheet to signify that you have seen this notice. Thank you for your cooperation.

Sincerely,

Jim Kelly
Social Studies Teacher

_____
Parent/Guardian Signature

CRITERIA FOR JUDGING PROJECTS

In your evaluation of the projects, consider the following criteria:

1. Adherence to theme (most important). The theme of this year's fair is

   _____

2. Adherence to rules.

3. Originality.

4. Creativity.

5. Workmanship.

6. Overall display, including background.

Awards will be presented for the following categories:

1. *Best in Fair.* This is the top award. Although there is no number limit for this award, winners should represent the cream of the crop. Recipients go on to the regional contest.

2. *Honorable Mention.* This award is for projects that are noteworthy but do not qualify for Best in Fair.

3. *Certificate of Participation.* Every student who participates receives this certificate.

THE COMMUNITY AS A RESOURCE

Can a school grow, independent of its surrounding community—especially in fiscally conservative days? Communities are treasure troves of information if only we know where to look.

Educators can draw community members closer to the schools, making them feel an integral part of the very special society they finance.

One way to do this is through a project I developed and am currently implementing called "Operation Talent Scout." Its objective is to tap into the talent that exists throughout the community. The cover letter that follows, together with a registration form, is sent to as many people in the community as possible. With the support of the local school board this material can be mailed to every member of the community. If that service is unavailable, it can be sent home with every student in the school system. Copies can also be placed in the local newspaper, banks, and libraries. And groups such as senior citizens and community business organizations can be contacted.

When the registration forms come in, it is a good idea to involve students, to let them feel a part of the process. For example, they can be organized to file the papers according to a prearranged system; better class time was never spent. If the service is available, you may be able to convince the superintendent that a computer printout of this information to be kept in the library would be an invaluable resource for each school building in the district, as well as a benefit for the community.

The community can also be used as a place of experimentation. I have had students research various town offices to create the ideal society in the classroom, among other things. Directions for one community activity—the "Soda Can Experiment"—follow.

Lastly, it is important to let the community know what you are doing. A good public relations committee in a school is of great value. Letting the public see and read about what is going on in the schools bodes well for the entire school district. Newspaper stories, fliers, and community newsletters represent only a part of this, however.

Parents need to feel that they can understand what is transpiring in each classroom. Indeed, they have a right to that information and it is incumbent upon us educators to provide them with it. Too often parents look upon a school as on any bureaucracy: too confusing, too many personalities, and too much going on at the same time to understand.

I suggest making a syllabus for parents. This may take the form of a brochure or of a few pages stapled together. If it becomes school policy, a collection of this material can be made into a booklet, which can be disseminated to parents at PTA meetings, sent home with their children, mailed, or given out at such functions as Back-to-School Night, Open House, or Parent-Teacher Conferences. Or it can even be available at public places like the local bank, supermarket, or town hall.

A sample of the class information I give to parents at our Back-to-School Night follows. It contains the title of the course, the objectives of the course, a list of materials used, the class requirements, and several suggestions to help parents better prepare their child for school.

Operation Talent Scout

LETTER

TO (THE PARENT/RELATIVE/FRIEND):

I am creating a valuable, educational file for the betterment of our school in which you might like to participate. It is entitled "Operation Talent Scout."

"Operation Talent Scout" will be the community resource program of the Richard Butler School. I believe there is a great deal of talent within our community that should not go to waste. I am sure there are many people with occupations, experiences, trips, special skills, or hobbies that they would like to share with the students in the schools.

This material could be shared by speaking to a single class or to a smaller group of children.

Those of you who wish to participate would be providing an extremely valuable service to your children and their teachers.

If you would like to be "on file" for "Operation Talent Scout," please complete the attached form and return it to our school with your son/daughter, mail it, or bring it to me here at school. The teacher who would like to make use of your knowledge will then contact you when the occasion arises.

Many thanks for your cooperation.

Sincerely,

Jim Kelley
Social Studies Teacher

(Do not write in this blank. Here you can key whatever filing system you have devised.)

NAME _____

ADDRESS _____

PHONE _____

AREA OF INTEREST _____

Please indicate in a few sentences a particular knowledge or skill you possess that you would like to share with the students of _____ School.

_____
_____
_____
_____
_____
_____
_____
_____

Please indicate in a sentence or two how you will present this knowledge or skill (for example, demonstration, lecture, slides).

_____
_____
_____
_____
_____
_____
_____
_____

Soda Can Experiment

PREPARATION

The object of this lesson is to provide students with an insight into how human beings react in a stressful situation.

Begin by selecting a group of five students to participate in the experiment. The selection of these students may be based on whatever criteria you wish to use—their appearance, their ability to act, their intelligence, or any of several other characteristics.

Then prepare a checklist to record the results of the experiment. On a sheet of ordinary, white, ruled paper, list the following categories:

1. No visible reaction
2. Body language
3. Picked up can
4. Verbal response
5. Other.

It will also be necessary to prepare students beforehand by making sure they understand the following terms: *human nature, body language, stress, insight, imply, infer, evaluate, generalization.*

THE EXPERIMENT

On a moderately temperate day, take your students and clipboard to the nearest shopping mall. (Since the weather may be a factor in the results of the experiment, choose a pleasant day when people won't be in a rush.) I use one of the three large supermarkets in our area because it allows for a constant flow of people. Explain to students what they are to do and where they are to position themselves. Don't let them know beforehand or the entire student body of the school will be there observing your observations.

Students are to do something quite simple. Three students position themselves near the entrance/exit to the supermarket and very near a trash can. In their possession is an empty soda can. As a customer comes out of the supermarket, the students laugh, talk loudly, and throw the can near, not at, the person.

Noting the reactions of the customers becomes the job of the other two students who remain with the teacher in a car parked nearby. Discuss the reaction of each customer, come to a consensus, and note it on the checklist. Some individuals will show no visible reaction, totally ignoring the situation, even though they are nearly hit with the can. Some will indicate their distaste by the use of body language: a dirty look, shaking the head, stopping and staring. Still others will merely pick up the can and throw it in the trash can. And a few will walk up to the students and verbally chastise them for their behavior. When a customer reacts in this way, the teacher should go over to the individual and explain the purpose of the activity. In my experience all such customers gained a renewed respect for adolescents and were pleased with our experiment.

Although these are the four general reactions usually encountered, there is a fifth category labeled "Other" for any unorthodox or unanticipated reaction. To date we have yet to record anything in this category.

Perform this experiment for an hour or so. Then discuss the results the following day in class. A lively, open discussion should ensue concerning the data amassed. Generalizations are implied by the information, but the students need to be made aware that hard, factual conclusions would be difficult to ascertain without a more detailed and scientific study. Nonetheless, the activity should stir their creative minds, encouraging them to think, analyze, and evaluate.

I. Title of Course: Eighth Grade Social Studies

II. Objectives

   A. It is hoped that upon completion of this course:

      1. Students will have an understanding of this country's history.

      2. Students will understand the role of our country in the world today.

      3. Students will have an understanding of the workings of our government.

      4. Students will be able to recognize the pitfalls of our country's past in order to avoid them in our nation's future.

      5. Students will realize that no system on earth is perfect, but that ours is best suited to our society and the individual.

      6. Students will be willing to effect change within the system we have rather than without.

   B. It is further hoped that upon completion of this course:

      1. Students will have a better understanding of themselves and the worth of their existence.

      2. Students will better understand their classmates and realize that they too are important.

      3. Foundations of prejudice will be removed.

      4. Students will realize that although their neighbor may not look, act, speak, or think the same as they do, each individual has worth and is deserving of their respect, if not affection.

   C. It is further hoped that, upon completion of this course, students will have had the opportunity to express their opinions on some of the major controversial issues of the day, as well as to share the thoughts of others.

   D. It is finally hoped that students will become strong in their ability to think as individuals, independent of bias, and then act accordingly.

III. Materials

   A. Text: *Let Freedom Ring* (Silver Burdett Co., 1977)

   B. *Values Clarification,* Simon, Howe, Kirschenbaum (Hart, 1972)

   C. Various supplementary materials: books, pamphlets, films, filmstrips

IV. Requirements

   A. Homework
   Homework will be given each day. It is the responsibility of the student to complete it according to classroom specifications and return it on time.

   B. Classwork
   Classwork will consist of writing essays, reading, role playing, discussion, group work, drawing, and independent projects.

   C. Tests and Quizzes
   Quizzes will be given with prior notice, to test the comprehension and listening capability of the student. Students will be quizzed on current events every week, and on text material periodically.
   Tests will be given with prior notice. Students are to create study guides and ample time will be allocated for review.

   D. History Fair
   Every eighth grader must complete a History Fair project.

   E. Group Work
   The eighth grade program stresses student participation. Students will be involved in various classtime projects that seek to use their skills and creativity.

V. Family

To help your children do better in school, please consider the following suggestions:

   A. Have a positive attitude toward school. Ask your children what they are doing and encourage them to do well.

   B. Oversee your children's homework. Make homework a priority. Be sure your children do their homework. Ask questions, discuss concepts, seek opinions, and give them off-the-cuff quizzes.

   C. Involve your children in doing projects independently. Students do many projects but all of these need not be initiated by the teacher. Look through the social studies book. Studying Egypt? Encourage your children to surprise the teacher and classmates with a model of King Tut's tomb.

   D. Screen the television programs your children watch. Television can and should be not only entertaining but educational. Watch with them and then discuss the programs.

   E. Take short day trips with your children. Discuss the trip beforehand. Find out in advance what you can about where you are going.

Trace the route on maps. On the way, make your child the navigator.

F. Play word games in the car. In short, make it an enjoyable and educational experience.

G. Encourage your children to be aware of the world around them. Make current events a priority. Discuss current events at the dinner table or afterward. Watch and discuss the news with your children.

H. To summarize, be interested, be involved, encourage project construction, make and interpret maps, and do whatever else you can think of to make the study of social studies fun and rewarding for your children.

UNINTENDED OUTCOMES

With any activity, unintended outcomes are often part of the baggage. All too often they are a neglected part. In a classroom that encourages divergent thinking, such outcomes take on new meaning.

I often ask students, on questionnaires and tests, what they think is the most important thing they have learned. Their responses are interesting, informative, and wide-ranging. Invariably, these answers give an insight into what really matters to a student. They also broaden the somewhat narrow objectives of a standard lesson for the teacher.

Some of the more interesting answers that I have collected from a series of tests follow.

Reactions to the Question: What Is the Most Important Thing You Have Learned?

The most important thing I have learned is—

- That school is more important than going out, because my education is more important than freedom to go out at night.
- That you could have fun in Social Studies because of the play the boys did in this class.
- That people are rarely treated fairly when it comes to world affairs, even if they are right.
- That machines make mistakes.
- That being a newscaster is hard.
- That fighting isn't as glorious as it may seem, because you don't always end up on top.
- That these presidents really are trying to help our country, it's just that it isn't working.
- Don't believe everything you hear or see.
- About propaganda—anybody would do anything to sell something, even lie about it.
- The devastation of war.
- That school isn't getting easier.

AFFECTIVE EDUCATION: SOME RESULTS

Much has been written about affective education; a great deal of it is misunderstood. Affective education is not, as its critics believe, an attempt to brainwash impressionable minds. It is, rather, an attempt to encourage children to feel as well as think.

To those who would do away with "values education," as affective education has been labeled, I would say that values are expressed in everything teachers do. From the pledge to the flag, to the way they dress and comb their hair, to the type of assignments they give, to the way in which they speak to their students, teachers are making a statement on values. The job of the competent instructor is to coordinate efforts in order to effectively teach the cognitive and affective areas.

Can teachers seriously teach about the rise of Nazism in Germany with an absence of values? Can they teach about pollution, read Shakespeare, view a van Gogh, listen to Mozart, and not expect their students to "feel"? Teachers can not only encourage their students to think and express their views as best as they can, they can also tap their ability to empathize, and help them analyze their feelings. In this way teachers are helping to perpetuate the human values traditionally found in our society.

A collection of values statements made by eighth graders follows. These are examples from the poems, stories, and essays students wrote describing their feelings after units on the Holocaust and the internment of Japanese–Americans during World War II. In reading them I hope you will discover, as I have, that affective education has its place in any subject, on any grade level, and our future is in goods hands.

Values Statements by Eighth Grade Students

POEM

Where have all the people gone?
Into the fiery inferno of hell.

So much destruction has been done,
yet Americans just shake their heads,
as if to say, "Oh, well."

My parents, sisters, cousins, and such,
have died at the hands of "brothers,"
All the people that meant so much,
mean nothing at all to others.

This world knows nothing of humanity,
for wars have killed us all,
Men have fought against human thoughts,
and I wish to break down this wall.

—Rebecca Ferring

AUSCHWITZ

The fire is out and the guns have stopped,
but the fires in minds are still lit.

People screaming, running, hiding,
afraid of a thing called death.

So many dead, so many scarred,
but not everyone who should be is behind bars.

Why the deaths of innocent people,
who never did anything wrong?

All those strong people who survived,
now sing that same old song.

That song of grief, of worry, of sadness,
a song of anger, a song of madness.

People left with that horrible scene,
that is worse than a bad dream.

Why did it start, why did it begin,
that terrible deadly sin?

The deaths and scene of gruesome fits
all happened in a death camp

Named Auschwitz.

—Jane Burt

HOLOCAUST

At dawn the people enter,
and they scream in horrified fright.

In a moment it's all over,
then the fire blazes bright.

In lands that aren't threatened,
the people sit content.

They know there is a Holocaust,
but help they haven't sent.

A few may not be worried,
they don't care for dying souls.

They know people are murdered,
and thrown in deep, dark holes.

One person may be worried,
or maybe quite a few,

But when an army rages,
what can one person do?

People must fight together,
all women and all men.

They have to save the dying ones,
and never let this happen again.

—Jaqueline Quinn

POEM

We read the signs, but could not believe
That they told us we had to leave.

We put all our things in a pack
And knew somehow we wouldn't be back.

They shipped us away, oh so far.
We ended up in Manzanar.

They split our families far and wide
And every night our children cried.

No one thought that it was fair.
They had no right to keep us there.

—Tom Pierce

POEM

Life has changed for Japanese–Americans.
Once they were free, and now they are not.
Like one who has become crippled,
They too have lost their mobility.
Bitterness and unhappiness have consumed their lives.
They remain in a cage, as a cripple
Is confined to a wheelchair:
Freedom seems unattainable.
Will they ever walk again?

—Jennifer VonSuskil

POEM

We started with something
And ended with nothing.
Our houses were sold; our belongings lost.
Our family life ruined.
The war is over and there is
Nothing to come home to.
What will happen to us?

—Jeff Barna

POEM

Paradise lost, paradise destroyed.
Pearl Harbor's bombs shattered harmony.
Mistrust grew out of the smoky rubble
Sending its ugly clouds to the land of the free.
''My country 'tis of thee'' no longer included
My Japanese sisters.
In our fear, we forgot liberty and justice for all,
Forcing my Japanese sisters into lives of insult and
   indignity.
Our ''home of the free and the brave''
No longer existed.
Now it was the land of the frenzied
Filled with prison fences.
We locked the doors and took away their freedom
   key—
In jobs, homes, and privacy,
Forgetting that America is a nation of everyone,
Not just a selected few.

               —Heather McCracken

CONCLUDING COMMENT

Teaching is a very hard job; at times it seems an impossibly difficult one. I suggest concentrating on what students can offer us as teachers. We survive on their energy; when a student exhibits original thought and creativity, our motivation thrives on it.

So, I offer a challenge. Reach out to your students as never before; strive to be as creative a teacher as possible. Such teaching will bring great rewards.

This publication ends with a poem written by a former student. Works such as this continually impress me with the capability of our youth.

PRIDE

A poem about leadership, values, and self-inflated importance.

Eighth grade was a breeze, and high school a wow,
But where are the great ones of yesterday now?
The jokes are all crippled, the cheerleaders gray,
The glory has faded, the fame's gone away.
They'd put anyone down just to get themselves high,
But now all the need for those games has gone by.
They all were the great ones—the kings of the school,
And making a joke out of someone was ''cool.''
But twenty years later, who are they, and where?
The fake smiles they had are no longer there.
For now they know something they should have known
   then,
False greatness will die, it's a matter of when.

               —Kathy Bulmer

BIBLIOGRAPHY

1. Adler, Mortimer J. *The Paideia Proposal.* New York: Macmillan Publishing Co., 1982.

2. Anderson, Harold H., ed. *Creativity and Its Cultivation.* New York: Harper and Bros., 1959.

3. Bailey, Gerald D. *Teacher Self-Esteem: A Means for Improving Classroom Instruction.* Washington, D.C.: National Education Association, 1981.

4. _____. *Teacher-Designed Student Feedback: A Strategy for Improving Classroom Instruction.* Washington, D.C.: National Education Association, 1983.

5. Cangelosi, James S. *Cooperation in the Classroom: Students and Teachers Together.* Washington, D.C.: National Education Association, 1984.

6. Coleman, James. *The Adolescent Society: The Social Life of the Teenager and Its Impact on Education.* New York: Free Press, 1961.

7. Henak, Richard M. *Lesson Planning for Meaningful Variety in Teaching.* 2d ed. Washington, D.C.: National Education Association, 1984.

8. Kenworthy, Leonard S. *Guide to Social Studies Teaching.* Belmont, Calif.: Wadsworth Publishing Co., 1970.

9. Lewis, Norman. *Word Power Made Easy.* New York: Pocket Books, 1973.

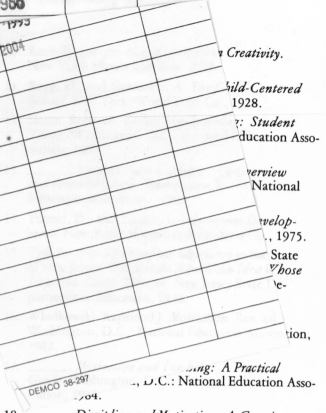

18. _____. *Discipline and Motivation: A Genuine Partnership.* Washington, D.C.: National Education Association, 1978. Audiocassettes.